Pakistan Travel Guide

A guide about Pakistan's Rich History & Tourism

Disclaimer and Copyright Notice

Table of Contents

Introduction

Pakistan has the world's 2nd largest Muslim population and it's strategically and geographically located in Asia. The first thing you need to know about Pakistan is the language. The country has many languages, including English, Urdu as well as Punjabi, Sindhi, Balochi and Pashto. Urdu is the national language of Pakistan. Although the language isn't always consistent, you should be able to communicate with the people you meet.

You can learn the local dialect and ask for help if you need it. You can also learn how to navigate your way around the country by asking the locals or using google maps. In addition to being able to speak Urdu and Punjabi, you should also be able to read Urdu. Once you've figured out the language, you'll be able to travel to Pakistan easily. The capital city is Islamabad, which is a bustling metropolis full of people and traffic. In the country, there are many scenic areas. There are green mountains, forests, and snow-capped peaks, and even a number of eye-catching routes.

Regardless of your destination, the people in Pakistan are very friendly and will do anything for you, whether it's free food, shelter, or a ride. In fact, most people will never ask for a tip, so don't be shy and ask if you can pay them a small fee. You'll be surprised by how generous people are and the kindness they have for tourists. It's worth the extra time and effort. This Pakistan travel guide will cover all the important information you'll need, from the best places to visit to the best ways to behave in the country. It will teach you how to get around and acclimatize to local life.

If you're wondering what the language is like, you can look at some local books or dictionaries on the internet. They will help you navigate your way through the language. The most important thing to know before you travel to Pakistan is that it's a Muslim nation and that it has a lot of Hindu, Sikh, Christian and Buddhist communities as well. The country is home to a variety of cultures, including many that share a common religion. You must avoid being too rude and don't talk back to locals.

A good example of how to behave is to use a tour guide. You can also use a local Pakistani travel guide to get around the country. The people of Pakistan are very welcoming and want to give you a warm welcome. The country is large, approximately 1.5 times larger than France. It borders Afghanistan, China, Iran and India. It shares a border with Tajikistan as well. Its maritime boundary is with Oman. It is strategically located on the sea, making it the perfect place for travelers to take their holidays. You'll feel safe and enjoy the landscape and culture.

There are a variety of ways to travel in Pakistan. Train services are the most common way to get from place to place. There are three different classes on trains: Economy class, berth, and Parlor. In 1st class, you'll have a long cushioned seat. Optional air conditioning is available in some departments. If you're traveling on a budget, you'll want to choose a seat in the first class. In addition to its rail system, Pakistan also has a vast road network.

There are budget flights to most major cities and a train to any part of the country. Whether you want to take a train or drive a car, you can find it easily in Pakistan. Just make sure that the route is suitable for you. You'll have to make sure that you don't get lost or miss any landmarks. You'll have to be careful in the country-side. There are no roads that are quite safe. Rather, you'll have to rely on public transport. Overall, the country is full of adventures and awesome tourist destinations.

Chapter 1: The Geography Of Pakistan

The Geography of Pakistan consists of four main regions: the north, East, West, and the south is dominated by the Arabian Sea. The northern highlands include the Karakoram and Pamir mountain ranges, which contain the highest mountains on Earth including K2. The southern region includes the Indus Plain, which is mostly flat. The northern highlands are characterized by rain and cool climates, and the Balochistan Plateau is characterized by hot summers.

Pakistan has four seasons, from cold to warm. The winter season lasts from October to February, followed by a pleasant spring from February to April, and a summer rainy season that lasts from May to September. The autumn monsoon period lasts from October to December. Although there are seasonal variations in each region, the climate varies from -10 degrees Celsius in January to forty degrees Celsius in June. The annual rainfall in Pakistan varies from less than ten centimeters to nearly 150 inches. The Indus plain is the largest and most fertile area of the subcontinent and is supported by the Indus River.

Pakistan's geographical landscape is dominated by the Himalayan range in the northwest, and by the coastal plains of the Arabian Sea in the south. The country also borders the Eurasian tectonic plate, which contains the largest mountain range, K-2. The northern mountains are characterized by the Potohar Plateau and the Balochistan plateau. The western plateaus contain salt deposits and are sparsely cultivated.

The mountains, deserts, and rivers make up the majority of the landmass in Pakistan. The highlands are divided by a large plateau, the Balochistan Plateau, and the Indus River plain. The north and eastern areas are covered by the Indus river and are supported by the mountains of the Indus Range. The mountain range is primarily located in the northern half of Pakistan. There are several rivers in Pakistan. The Punjab and the Indus River valley are the most common geographic regions of Pakistan. The country's climate is hot and humid, and it has a range of different types of climates. The climatic conditions in a few regions are very different from the climate in the rest of the country. The mountains of the Indus Range are also quite variable, which is why it's important to know the local weather conditions in each region.

The climate in Pakistan varies. There are four distinct seasons in Pakistan. Winters are mild in the north and dry in the south. The country's climate is temperate, while the winters are chilly in the southern plains. The country has a very diverse range of landscapes and terrain. Unlike many other countries in Asia, it is mainly an arid and semi-arid country with high mountains. While Pakistan has many natural features, it is also home to wild cats, dogs, birds, elephants and other species. Indus river dolphins and mugger crocodiles are famous in the country, while the vast majority of species are found in the northern part of the country.

The climate of Pakistan is characterized by extreme temperature fluctuations. The mountains of the northwestern part of the country are extremely cold, and the plains of the Indus Valley are hot and dry. The coastal region has a more temperate climate. Its mountain ranges are more than a thousand meters high, with the highest peak being in the Karakoram.

1.1 Cities in Pakistan

There are many places to visit in Pakistan, but the most important thing is to choose the right city. Islamabad, the capital city, is a beautiful place to visit, and the people are friendly and hospitable. There are also plenty of beautiful mountains and natural attractions to explore in this country. Planning your trip is essential to ensure your safety and enjoyment. You should be aware of the different security measures in place, and make a checklist of things you want to do before you leave.

The cities of Pakistan are divided into four provinces: Punjab, Balochistan, KPK, and Sindh. While Azad Jammu & Kashmir and Gilgit Baltistan are also part of Pakistan and under their administration. The largest city is Abbottabad. The second largest is Lahore, which is located in the central region. Rawalpindi is nine miles from the national capital Islamabad. The population of Rawalpindi is approximately 1,000,000. It is home to several large companies, including the government's Information Technology Division. It also boasts a diverse cultural scene with many festivals and events.

The three major cities in Pakistan are Islamabad, Lahore, and Karachi. The first one, Islamabad, is a super-sleek metropolis with world-class cultural attractions and contemporary architecture. The second city, Lahore, is an ancient city with Mughal architecture and UNESCO World Heritage Sites. There are also six cities in Pakistan with populations of one million or more.

For a comprehensive list of cities in Pakistan, look no further than the World Gazetteer Online. The online directory, World Gazetteer Online, features information on every city in the country. The search results for each city are organized by region, and the results are returned based on geographic coordinates. Once you've decided which city best suits your needs and interests, you're ready to plan your next trip. Another largest city in Pakistan, Karachi, is a cosmopolitan and multicultural city. It is home to more non-Muslim religious communities than any other city in Pakistan. Its residents are diverse, with groups from all over the country, from nearby countries, and from the western world. Therefore, visitors to the city will experience different cultures and lifestyles. Whether you're interested in history, culture, or religion, you'll find a destination in Pakistan that best suits your needs.

While many travelers choose a city in Pakistan for its mountainous landscapes, it's still important to stay safe while traveling. There are many reasons to visit Pakistan, and its cities are as varied as its people. The country's vast mountainous areas and a number of cities have a rich history, and it is important to remember that the best places to visit in Pakistan are safe for travelers. The most visited cities in the country are the ones where the mountains are. You can hire a private guide in Pakistan, but it can be difficult to find a good guide who is knowledgeable. Taxi services are often expensive, so make sure you have enough cash on hand to pay for a driver. When it comes to public transportation, you can use local buses, taxis, and Uber or Careem. The latter is convenient and cheap and you may even be able to share the ride with other travelers. It's important to know that there are no rules or regulations regarding taxis in Pakistan.

While traveling in Pakistan, you should be aware of the risks and precautions associated with the country. There are many dangerous areas to visit, so make sure to plan your trip carefully and follow the instructions of law enforcement officers. It's also important to avoid overheating and drinking alcohol when traveling alone. There are many popular cities in the country, including Faisalabad and Rawalpindi. If you're traveling to Pakistan for a vacation, you can make use of the country's major highways and cities. You'll be surprised by how many great places you'll discover in this small country! And with so many options, you'll never be bored!

1.2 Things to do in Pakistan

If you are looking for fun things to do in Pakistan, you have come to the right place! There are plenty of fun things to do in Pakistan, and you will find it impossible not to enjoy them all! Here are some ideas for your trip to Pakistan. First, let's talk about its population. At just over 227 million people, it is the fifth most populous country in the world. In fact, it has the second largest Muslim population in the world. The country is also the third largest by area, measuring 881,913 square kilometers.

While you're in Pakistan, make sure to visit the Mohenjo-Daro site. You can see structures from one of the world's oldest civilizations. These monuments date back to 2500 BC, and they're a must-see in the country. While you're here, you'll have a chance to experience some Pakistani hospitality.

If you're interested in history and culture, you should visit the Museum of Natural History. This museum is dedicated to the study of zoology, botany, and earth sciences. The replicas in the Museum will teach you about the evolution of plants and animals in Pakistan. You'll learn about the country's geology and paleontology from the permanent exhibits. Once you've seen the exhibits, head to the city's markets to shop.

The cultural capital of Pakistan is the city of Islamabad. Here, you can visit the famous Lal Masjid, or "red mosque." The mosque is covered with red bricks, and it stands out from the many mosques in Islamabad. It's a great place to pray and is surrounded by lush greenery. It's also a great place to relax after a long day at work. A must-do in Pakistan is visiting the Lal Masjid. This iconic building translates to "red mosque." The red bricks on the exterior of the structure make it stand out among other mosques, and it is a beautiful place to worship. You can even visit the Rakaposhi glacier, which is the highest point in Pakistan. The city is famous for its breathtaking views of the mountain. You can spend hours just gazing at the landscape and taking pictures of the various ruins.

If you love shopping, the city of Islamabad is the perfect place to visit. The Centaurus has everything you'll need, from top restaurants to designer clothes and electronics. It's also the perfect place to meet the locals. For a truly stunning view of Islamabad, head to the Daman-e-Koh viewpoint. This city is also home to yaks and a number of high-altitude lakes. The location is great for sightseeing and is an ideal place to visit for lunch. If you're traveling on a budget, you can sample authentic Pakistani cuisine in a nearby cafe. You can also enjoy some great local drinks in the city.

During the holidays, you can spend time exploring the Kalasha region and experiencing their culture. The Kalash people live in three valleys in Chitral district. They have their own unique culture and religion. Their women wear colorful head-dresses and wear colorful hats. They have their own language and religious beliefs, and they celebrate their festivals in a way that will delight children and adults alike. The festival is held in the summer, but you can visit anytime during the year for a taste of their food.

If you want to experience the culture of the Kalash people, you can visit their villages in Pakistan. The Kalash people are a Dardic tribe, and are believed to be descended from the deserters of Alexander The Great. They celebrate their festivals in an ancient cave, and women wear colorful head-dresses. Their costumes are colorful and they enjoy libations more than most other Pakistanians. To visit the village, you can book a tour with a local tour operator and see their unique culture and traditions.

If you want to experience the culture of the people of Pakistan, you should visit the monument. Its architecture is beautiful, and its main goal is to commemorate the history of the country. It is reminiscent of flowers and displays the traditional Mughal architecture. The monument is a great place to visit with your family, as it shows the pride you have for your country. There are also many fun and interesting things to do in Pakistan.

You should also consider visiting the city of Lahore. The capital of the Punjab province, Lahore is home to some of the country's most spectacular architecture. You should visit the UNESCO-listed Shalimar Gardens and the Badshahi Mosque. The latter is an impressive example of Mughal architecture and rivals the Taj Mahal in beauty. The city's Gate of Chauburji is an excellent example of ancient Mughal history. And if you're hungry, you should head to Gawalmandi Food Street and sample some of the finest dishes in the city.

1.3 Pakistan's Geography And Climate

Geographically, Pakistan's climate is temperate, characterized by extreme temperature variations. The northern mountains are covered with ice and experience arctic conditions, while the coastal plains receive abundant rainfall. As a result, temperature differences are very large within the country, with daily variations ranging from eleven to seventeen degrees Celsius. In winter, temperatures drop to minus ten degrees, and snow is a common occurrence.

Pakistan's climate is a continental climate, with two distinct seasons. Summers are extremely hot and rainy, while winters are cold and dry. The monsoon season is mild, extending between April and August. In the north, the temperatures are relatively cool, but snow may fall at any time, and winters can be extremely cold. Even in the southern mountains, winter temperatures can be sub zero in some regions.

The climate of Pakistan is diverse and varies considerably. Mountainous areas in the northwestern part of the country are cold and dry throughout the year. In the south, the coast offers a moderate climate and a coastal strip. There is a general lack of precipitation in the country, with an average annual rainfall of sixteen centimeters in northern areas of the lower Indus plains to more than 120 centimeters in the Himalayan area.

The topography of Pakistan varies. The country has a mountainous north and a flat indus plain. The north of the country is largely mountainous, and it is characterized by hot and humid summers. The northwest has a very cold winter, but in the east, the climate is temperate. The prevailing temperature is warm and dry. During summer, the temperature can reach as high as fifty degrees.

Chapter 2: Cuisine, Culture & Planning A Trip

2.1 Eating & Drinking

Pakistan is an ideal destination for a foodie vacation. The cuisine is a mix of Indian and Pakistani influences. The mainstays of Pakistani cuisine are kebabs, curries, and salads. The carbohydrate portion of the meal is usually made up of flatbread and rice. The country's unique cultural background has resulted in a range of dishes with distinctive tastes.

Many people choose to make vegetarian meals during their travels to Pakistan, primarily due to the availability of fresh vegetables. Meat is commonly used in Indian-style cooking. Vegetables include okra, cabbage, and bitter gourd. Spicy dishes are topped with tandoori sauce and topped with cheese. Vegetables also make an excellent meal. If you're visiting Pakistan for the first time, be sure to try a variety of dishes.

Haleem is a popular dish in Pakistan. Made with barley, local wheat varieties, and chana, haleem is a traditional, hearty dish that highlights the Middle East's influence on the cuisine. It takes up to a day to cook and is served with bread and a side of fresh fruit. Traditionally, this dish is flavored with onions, green chilies, and masala spices and garnished with lemon juice.

The staples of Pakistani food are rice, wheat-based flatbread, lentils, vegetables, and yogurt. In addition to rice, you can also eat meat, poultry, and fish. In Pakistan, you can even find grilled chicken, lamb, and lamb. Most people enjoy halva puri for breakfast. For dinner, you can expect rice, nuts, and stewed protein dishes. When you visit Pakistan, you'll find the locals eating this way.

A meal in Pakistan is a cultural experience that should be shared. You'll have the opportunity to sample a variety of dishes and discover the various flavors of the country. In Pakistan, the staple food is rice, but there are also many types of bread. A popular dish is the halwa puri. A variety of other meats are also available. In addition to the halva, you'll probably have a lot of choices for dessert.

Karahi is one of the most iconic dishes of Pakistan. It is a dish that is beloved by every Pakistani. You can find a karahi dish in any small shop, or even in the palatial kitchen of a local Rajah. The dish is named after its black iron scoop-shaped pan. The main ingredients of a karahi curry are usually chicken, goat, or shrimp, cooked in oil and then mixed together. The meal is served with rice, roti, and a metal serving dish.

There are several types of traditional Pakistani food. The most popular is biriyani, which is served with hot roti bread. This dish is oily and meaty and is often very slimy. Its appearance is similar to that of pulao, but it is different. In a pulao, all of the ingredients are cooked together in oil. In a biryani, the ingredients are separated and fried together, making it very different from the aforementioned dish.

The rice is fried separately. This makes it very thin and crispy. This dish is served with a spicy and aromatic chickpea curry. For breakfast, you can enjoy the traditional biryani. Pakistan's cuisine is a blend of Indian and Mughal cuisines. Vegetarian food is very popular in Pakistan and dishes are made with spices from both countries. Chili's, turmeric, garlic, and fenugreek seeds are some of the common spices in Pakistani cooking. Vegetable dishes are also popular in Pakistan. Most of the meals are made with meat, but vegetarians can enjoy the same types of foods.

2.2 Health Issues And How To Prevent

Travel to Pakistan without immunization can expose you to a range of health risks. Although most countries recommend this, Pakistan is a particularly good destination for travelers. People should be fully vaccinated before traveling, and the country's low immunization coverage is associated with negative socio-economic factors and conflict. The geography of Pakistan presents many challenges, including the Himalayan mountain range and glaciers in the north, and the sparsely populated Balochistan province.

Fortunately, the military has opened up more of the controlled areas in recent months, but it is still important to visit the WHO's travel health website for updated information. It is also advisable to get a malaria vaccine for children who are traveling internationally. The CDC recommends that unvaccinated people receive COVID-19 vaccines before traveling overseas. Hepatitis B vaccinations are recommended for all ages, but do not count towards the routine 2-dose series. If you have any allergies, consider getting an immunoglobulin vaccine, which will protect you against malaria for two months.

The Department of State also recommends that travelers get vaccinated against COVID-19. Depending on your age, you may need to get several doses of this vaccine, but it can help reduce your risk of contracting the disease. CDC's website provides more information on COVID-19 and how to prevent it before traveling abroad. If you're unsure of the recommended vaccinations, consider getting a medical consultation from your doctor before travelling to Pakistan.

There are several health problems you'll encounter while visiting Pakistan. The most important one is drug addiction. Despite the fact that the country is not as dangerous as many travelers think, it still has a high incidence of drugs and is a significant problem. The CDC has warned travelers to be aware of COVID-19 and other health issues before travelling to Pakistan.

In Pakistan, food insecurity is a major contributor to poverty. The World Food Programme estimates that one in two people in Pakistan suffers from food insecurity. During the Great Partition, the country was split into two, and since then, the country's population has been displaced. It's also a poor and unstable country. Its people live in a rural area with few opportunities to travel.

The most common health issues in Pakistan are due to poverty. According to the World Food Programme, one out of every hundred citizens of Pakistan suffers from severe food insecurity. Moreover, the rapid urbanization of the country and the poor infrastructure in rural areas has created a wide range of health problems. Among these are sex-based crimes and violence. In addition to these, you should be aware of the risk of terrorism. In addition, polio issues can be observed, with the country having the highest rate of diabetes in South Asia. Further, there are several major cancer hospitals in Pakistan. If you suspect that a certain illness is on your way, you'll want to be aware of the risk and take steps to avoid it. The best way to prevent the disease is to contact a health care provider before you go.

2.3 Planning A Trip To Pakistan

There are many reasons why you should plan a trip to Pakistan, but the main reason is safety. Because Pakistan is a predominantly male country, it can be difficult to meet local women. It is also important to be aware of the culture before you visit. While it may seem different from other countries, Pakistan is an incredibly safe place to travel.

Getting around the country is not difficult, but you should prepare for a rough ride. There are many cities to explore in Pakistan. You'll need to carry a fair amount of cash, as the country is not yet paperless. However, you can find a lot of cheap accommodations in major cities. It can be useful to join a Backpacking Pakistan Facebook group to get information and meet other travelers.

If you're planning on traveling to Pakistan by plane, you should consider traveling with good companies. It's more affordable and you'll be able to see the country's ethnic diversity. Moreover, you won't need to worry about terrorism since the government has strict policies about it and Police & Army are very active to control it. In addition, you can get to Pakistan by air, but make sure you plan your trip in advance. Most travelers don't need visas, but if you are staying with relatives or visiting small towns or rural areas, you should consider getting vaccinations. If you are prone to adventure eating, you should also consider bringing along some anti-allergic drugs.

First, you should check the country's visa requirements. You should make sure that you are not infected with Covid-19 if you're planning to travel to Pakistan. It's also essential that you know the best way to reach your destination safely and legally. Secondly, obtaining a visa for Pakistan is important for safety. It's vital to make sure that you are traveling in a safe manner to avoid getting robbed, and to avoid any type of harm to yourself.

The country's security is one of its main attractions. It's a growing country, and security checks are common. While there are armed forces, the government is constantly checking the borders with neighbors. Having a visa is the only way to enter the country, so be sure to plan a trip to the country beforehand. You'll also need to carry at least 10 passport photos and a few other valuable documents. You'll want to make sure that you're properly vaccinated. You'll need to take the Hepatitis A and B vaccines. Vaccination is an essential part of preventing the spread of diseases in Pakistan. While the government tries to protect the people, it's not always safe. If you're traveling to Pakistan on a budget, you'll want to avoid the worst possible time to travel. Holiday season is usually very costly.

Although Urdu is the official language of Pakistan, there are many other regional languages spoken in the country. The Sindhi, Gowri, and Pashto are just a few of the many languages you'll encounter in Pakistan. While the national language is the most widely used, the other languages are more common in respective local areas. While the country's economy is thriving, the country's political stability and religious beliefs remain a concern. If you're planning a trip to Pakistan, it's important to be prepared for possible emergencies.

2.4 Climate & Where To Stay

If you are planning to travel in Pakistan, you should know what to expect from the weather. The climate varies across the country, with winters being very cold and snowy. Mountainous areas are inaccessible in winter, but can be easily visited between April and November. Cherry blossoms are in bloom during this time, and fall colors can be seen from mid-to-late December. It is recommended to pack light and pack your own pillow and blanket.

In cities, you can find good hotels. If you travel outside the Swat Valley, Chitral, or Northern areas, you might have trouble finding accommodation. Couch surfing is very popular in larger cities. If you want to meet other travelers, you can join the Backpacking Pakistan Facebook group. The members of the group are a great resource for travel information and tips. Also, you can meet people in this forum. There are many cities in Pakistan, but if you travel solo, you may find it challenging to find decent accommodations. You can find it inside or outside of the North-West Frontier Province, the Swat Valley, and the Karakoram Mountains. If you don't mind staying with a local, try Couchsurfing. You'll be able to meet fellow travelers and get information about the best places to stay in Pakistan while travelling.

While it can be difficult to find accommodations outside of the northern areas, Pakistan's many cities are worth exploring. You can easily get off the beaten path by staying in one of the more remote towns. Visiting the Ghizer District can help you discover rural regions where few tourists visit. The bluest lakes and peaceful ambiance in the Yasin Valley will transport you back in time. The Yasin Valley and Phander Valley are two locations where you can enjoy the best of Pakistan's landscape.

Choosing the right place to stay in Pakistan is a crucial decision. The country has a diverse population and has a relatively simple culture. However, the security situation has improved dramatically in recent years. If you are planning to travel to the Northern Areas, you should prepare for a wild ride! Aside from the natural beauty of the landscape, you will also enjoy the warm hospitality of the locals. There are a number of important things to consider when planning a visit to Pakistan. If you are planning to travel to Pakistan with your family, you should keep the safety of your children in mind. In addition to the country's security and safety issues, Pakistan is an officially developing country.

Security in Pakistan is a major concern. The country's security situation has improved significantly in recent years, and it is safe to travel to Pakistan in general. The country's border with India is still quite volatile, so you should make sure to stay away from it if you are visiting the country without your family. While it is possible to get around safely, you must trust your instincts and don't forget to carry identification with you. Women should be aware of the risks of traveling alone. The security situation is under control, it is essential to travel with a companion. Remember to have a travel insurance plan and avoid traveling alone. In addition to your security, you should also be aware of the local culture. Some countries are very liberal, while others have strict rules on how to behave in public.

While you are traveling, you must be aware of the safety risks associated with your travels. While Pakistani women are generally considered safe and respected, it is still wise to wear a head covering and cover your shoulders when visiting religious sites. If you are visiting the country's border regions, you should make sure that you have permission from the local authorities. Further, if you are a female, it is okay to poke your head in the kitchen and introduce yourself to the family.

2.5- 5 Cities You Must Visit When Travelling Pakistan

1.Lahore

Lahore is the capital city of the Punjab province in Pakistan. It is the second largest city in Pakistan, the 26th largest in the world, and one of the wealthiest in the country. It is home to several museums and other historical attractions that make the city a must-see for visitors.

The City's vibrant culture is a great example of multiculturalism. Its colorful streets are full of life and a lively nightlife will make you feel at home. You can also visit the shrine of Madho lal Hussain to learn about the Sufi faith, which is a form of Islam. In Lahore, there are many Muslim mosques and Hindu Mandirs. You must visit the Anarkali Bazaar. This is the oldest bazaar in Lahore and features a large tomb with a fascinating backstory. You can also try the puri in Lahore.

If you're planning to visit Lahore for its culture and history, you must wear proper clothing. The Orange Line metro has been opened as well, so if you're going to visit the city, make sure to take advantage of this service. Otherwise, you'll have to walk.

2. Karachi

With beautiful beaches and modern life Karachi is a must to visit place on your trip. The city busy life and modern shopping malls creates a unique experience specially the food is mindblowing as well.

Karachi offers a multi cultural city having residents from all offer Pakistan and often reffered to 'Mini Pakistan'

3. Islamabad

The Capital City of Pakistan is a must visit tourist destination as it has been ranked as 2nd most beautiful capital in the world. The mesmerizing landscape and beautiful mountains creates a serene environment.

4. Hunza

Hunza ranked as one of the most exotic tourist destination recently is a valley of heaven with amazing lakes, mountains and beautiful people and along with amazing food as well.

5. Skardu

Skardu is a natural wonder with beautiful lakes surrounded by mountains creating a mesmerizing experience for the visitor. The shangrilla resort shall be the ideal place to stay during the visit.

Conclusion

As a travel writer, I was curious about the country's culture and history. I knew that Pakistan was a complex place with many cultures and ethnic groups. Then, I read several books about Pakistan, including The Age of Kali by William Dalrymple, which contains several chapters about Pakistan. I was interested in the country's culture and history, and I wanted to find a travelling guide that would provide me with the necessary information to get the most out of my visit.

One of the major problems of male travelers is meeting women in Pakistan. It is very difficult to meet women in Pakistan, and most of them are shy or unwilling to do discussions. In addition, it is very rude to talk about your girlfriend in public. Many women stay away from foreigners, and Pakistanis get angry easily if you try to flirt with them. However, if you're travelling with a girlfriend, the culture of Pakistan is much more accepting. They won't shame you for having a girlfriend. The best way to meet women in the country is to ask them for permission. You can avoid unnecessary inconvenience and delays by planning your trip in advance. Before you leave the country, draw up a tentative itinerary. You can also consult with local guides or dedicated online groups. It is recommended to get a No Objection Certificate before visiting some locations. You may want to hire local drivers and guides to help you navigate the country. The majority of tourists visit Punjab. The rest of the country also has a real culture and people are friendly.

While there are many things to look forward to in Pakistan, the most important thing is to remember that it is an eastern world. If you're traveling alone, you will most likely encounter confusion and discomfort as you try to make friends. Getting a visa to Pakistan is not difficult, but you will need to have an itinerary in mind. A good guide will have a map that shows you the areas of the country you're planning to visit and what you need to know. You can also search for local information on Facebook and plan your trip yourself. If you have time and money, you can also join groups where travelers are planning a trip.

Despite the fact that Pakistan is a peaceful country, it is also a beautiful and diverse country. Its remoteness and lack of tourism infrastructure makes it a fantastic place for adventure seekers. You can do everything from climbing to hiking in the mountains. If you are the adventurous type, you can also check out the local cuisine and enjoy some local entertainment. Aside from the culture, you can even get a taste of the local food in the nearby towns. There are various ways of getting around in Pakistan. The most common is by bus or train, though rickshaws are the most popular form of transportation. Depending on your destination, you can hire a cab or use a rickshaw. There are also many buses and jeeps, but these options can be overwhelming. Luckily, there are well-run Daewoo and Faisal Movers services to help you get around the country. Taking the train is the best option for long-distance travel in Pakistan. While trains are relatively comfortable, it is important to research the routes before you hop on. Besides, train routes in Pakistan are often unpaved and not well-maintained. So, always plan your journey accordingly. It is a good idea to make the most of your time in this country.

Thankyou for Reading!

Please review us and subscribe at

www.booksclub.org

www.ingramcontent.com/pod-product-compliance
Ingram Content Group UK Ltd.
Pitfield, Milton Keynes, MK11 3LW, UK
UKHW022008190726
13853UKWH00004B/1818

9 798424 086915